THE BILL OF RIGHTS
in Translation
What It Really Means

by Amie Jane Leavitt

Consultant:
Philip Bigler
Director, The James Madison Center
James Madison University
Harrisonburg, Virginia

Capstone *press*

Mankato, Minnesota

Fact Finders is published by Capstone Press,
151 Good Counsel Drive, P.O. Box 669, Mankato, Minnesota 56002.
www.capstonepub.com

Library of Congress Cataloging-in-Publication Data
Leavitt, Amie Jane.
The Bill of Rights in translation : what it really means / by Amie Jane Leavitt.
    p. cm. — (Fact finders. Kids' translations)
    Includes bibliographical references and index.
    Summary: "Presents the Bill of Rights in both its original version and in a translated version using everyday
language. Describes the events that led to the creation of the document and its significance through history" — Provided by
publisher.
    ISBN-13: 978-1-4296-1928-8 (hardcover)
    ISBN-13: 978-1-4296-2843-3 (softcover pbk.)
    ISBN-13: 978-1-4296-5951-2 (saddle-stitched)
    1. United States. Constitution. 1st–10th Amendments. 2. Civil rights — United States — History. 3. Constitutional
amendments — United States — History. I. Title. II. Series.
    KF4750.L43 2009
    342.7308'5 — dc22
                                                                                  2007051307

Editorial Credits
Megan Schoeneberger, editor; Gene Bentdahl, set designer and illustrator; Wanda Winch, photo researcher

Photo Credits
Alamy/Wayne Grundy, 4
Blue Earth County Sheriff's Office, Mankato, Minnesota, 11 (left)
Capstone Press/Karon Dubke, cover (girl), 7 (top), 11 (right), 28
Department of Special Collections of the University Libraries of Notre Dame, 17 (coins)
Getty Images Inc./Alex Wong, 25; The Bridgeman Art Library, 23 (top); The Bridgeman Art Library/George Peter
    Alexander Healy, cover; Hulton Archive/MPI, 20–21; Stock Montage, 9 (left)
Jones Memorial Library, Lynchburg, Virginia, 7 (bottom)
Library of Congress, 14, 16
Library of Congress Manuscript Division, 23 (bottom)
Manhattan Rare Book Company, 9 (right)
National Archives and Records Administration (NARA)/General Records of the U.S. Government Group 11, Engrossed
    Bill of Rights, 4 (right), 6 (right); Charters of Freedom, 18, 19
North Wind Picture Archives, 6, 8, 10, 22,
Shutterstock/Rafa Irusta, 12
SuperStock Inc./SuperStock, 5
Wikimedia, 17 (bills)

Note: Essential content terms are **bold** and are defined at the bottom of the page where they first appear.

Printed in China
092010   005944

Table of Contents

CHAPTER 1

The Bill of Rights
WHAT'S THE BIG DEAL?

Imagine having no rights. The government tells you what you can or can't say. You can't choose your religion. The government controls what newspapers and magazines print. If you complain, you get thrown into jail. You could be locked up for years without ever getting a trial.

Thanks to the Bill of Rights, Americans don't have to worry about losing their rights. The Bill of Rights is the first 10 **amendments** to the Constitution. These amendments list rights that belong to all Americans.

amendment — a change that is made to a law or constitution

The Bill of Rights protects citizens of the United States. You don't have to be wealthy or powerful. The Bill of Rights protects all citizens, even you.

Congress OF THE United States

begun and held at the City of New York, on Wednesday the Fourth of March, one thousand seven hundred and eighty nine

What exactly do each of these amendments mean to you? Turn to the next page to find out.

CHAPTER 2

The Bill of Rights
WHAT IT MEANS

The Bill of Rights
Amendment I

Congress shall make no law respecting an establishment of religion, or prohibiting the free exercise thereof; or abridging the freedom of speech, or of the press; or the right of the people peaceably to assemble, and to petition the Government for a redress of grievances.

In some other countries, the government tells the citizens what religion to follow. Many people have come to America to be able to worship as they please.

What?

First Amendment:

You can say or write just about anything you want. You can follow any **religion** you choose. People can gather in groups. And if you have **complaints** about the government, go ahead and speak up. The government can't stop you.

Before 1776, Great Britain ruled the 13 U.S. colonies. During that time, colonists could be thrown in jail for criticizing the government.

newspaper, 1795

The Bill of Rights Continued

Amendment II

A well regulated **Militia**, being necessary to the security of a free State, the right of the people to keep and bear Arms, shall not be **infringed**.

Amendment III

No Soldier shall, in time of peace be quartered in any house, without the consent of the Owner, nor in time of war, but in a manner to be prescribed by law.

infringed — taken away or lessened

militia — an armed force made up of citizens who are trained to fight but who are called to serve only in emergencies

What?

Second Amendment:

To protect the country, citizens sometimes must serve as **soldiers**. Citizens also have a right to protect themselves. The government can't stop people from owning guns.

Third Amendment:

Soldiers can't **barge in** and demand to live in your house and eat your food.

In the 13 colonies, militias were groups of citizens called minutemen. They were ordinary men trained and ready to fight at a minute's notice.

If British soldiers demanded it, colonists had to let them sleep in their beds and eat their food. This was called quartering soldiers.

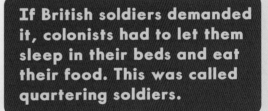

the Quartering Act of 1774

The Bill of Rights Continued

Amendment IV

The right of the people to be secure in their persons, houses, papers, and effects, against unreasonable searches and **seizures**, shall not be violated, and no Warrants shall issue, but upon **probable cause**, supported by Oath or affirmation, and particularly describing the place to be searched, and the persons or things to be seized.

probable cause — a reason that is likely to be true

seizure — the act of taking hold of or capturing somebody or something

Fourth Amendment:

Police can't just walk into your house, search through your stuff, and take it away. First, they need to get a **search warrant**. And for that, they must give a really good reason for the search. They also have to say exactly where they want to search and what they are looking for.

Courts issue search warrants.

APPLICATION 1-1

COURT

APPLICATION FOR SEARCH WARRANT AND SUPPORTING AFFIDAVIT.

STATE OF MINNESOTA, COUNTY OF

STATE OF MINNESOTA) SS.
COUNTY OF)

, being first duly sworn upon oath, hereby makes application to this Court for a warrant to search the hereinafter described, for the property and things hereinafter described.

Affiant knows the contents of this application and supporting affidavit, and the statements herein are true of his/her own knowledge, save as to such as are herein stated on information and belief, and as to those, he/she believes them to be true.

Affiant has good reason to believe, and does believe, that the following described property and things, to wit:

will be described as:

located in the of , County of , and State of Minnesota.

This Affiant applies for issuance of a search warrant upon the following grounds:

The Bill of Rights Continued

Amendment V

No person shall be held to answer for a capital, or otherwise infamous crime, unless on a presentment or indictment of a **Grand Jury**, except in cases arising in the land or naval forces, or in the Militia, when in actual service in time of War or public danger; nor shall any person be subject for the same offence to be twice put in jeopardy of life or limb; nor shall be compelled in any criminal case to be a witness against himself, nor be deprived of life, liberty, or property, without due process of law; nor shall private property be taken for public use, without just compensation.

grand jury — a group of people that meet to decide if there is enough evidence to try someone for a crime

Capital crimes are really serious crimes that could call for the death penalty.

A grand jury is a group of 12 to 23 citizens.

Fifth Amendment:

For a **capital crime**, a **grand jury** has to decide if there is enough evidence to charge you. You can be **charged only once** for a crime. If you are found not guilty, you can't be tried again. In court, you don't have to **say anything against yourself**. Nobody can take away your life, freedom, or belongings without giving you a fair trial first. And if the government takes any of your stuff, they have to pay you for it.

Being charged twice for the same crime is called "double jeopardy." The Bill of Rights makes double jeopardy illegal.

Choosing not to answer questions during your own trial is called "taking the fifth." This right is guaranteed by the Fifth Amendment.

13

The Bill of Rights Continued
Amendment VI

In all criminal prosecutions, the accused shall enjoy the right to a speedy and public trial, by an **impartial** jury of the State and district wherein the crime shall have been committed, which district shall have been previously ascertained by law, and to be informed of the nature and cause of the accusation; to be confronted with the witnesses against him; to have compulsory process for obtaining witnesses in his favor, and to have the Assistance of Counsel for his defense.

a jury trial in 1800

impartial — fair

Sixth Amendment:

If you're charged with a crime, your trial should happen as soon as possible. You shouldn't sit in jail **for years** waiting for a trial. Your trial must be held in public. It can't be kept secret. At the trial, a jury will decide if you are guilty or innocent. The government has to tell you exactly what you are accused of and who is making charges against you. You have the right to tell your side of the story in court. You can have a **lawyer** and witnesses to back you up.

In some other countries, people can be locked up for no given reason. They often wait in jail for years before they finally get a trial. Sometimes, they don't get a trial at all.

If you cannot afford a lawyer, the government has to provide one for you.

The Bill of Rights Continued

Amendment VII

In Suits at common law, where the value in controversy shall exceed twenty dollars, the right of trial by jury shall be preserved, and no fact tried by a jury, shall be otherwise re-examined in any Court of the United States, than according to the rules of the common law.

Amendment VIII

Excessive **bail** shall not be required, nor excessive fines imposed, nor cruel and unusual punishments inflicted.

bail — a fee you pay to get out of jail until your trial

What?

Civil cases involve disputes over money or property, not crimes.

Seventh Amendment:

You can have a jury settle **civil cases** involving **a lot of money**. Once the case is decided, it can't be brought up again in another court.

Eighth Amendment:

Your punishment should fit your crime. You shouldn't have to pay too much bail or unreasonable fines. The government can't punish you in a cruel or unusual way.

Back in 1791, $20 was a lot of money. The average person had to work 40 days to earn that much.

People shouldn't spend the rest of their lives in jail just for stealing bread from a store. If people speed in their car, they shouldn't get a $50,000 fine.

coins and bills from the late 1700s

The Bill of Rights Continued

Amendment IX

The enumeration in the Constitution, of certain rights, shall not be construed to deny or disparage others retained by the people.

Amendment X

The powers not delegated to the United States by the Constitution, nor prohibited by it to the States, are reserved to the States respectively, or to the people.

The Missing Amendments

The original draft of the Bill of Rights had 12 amendments. What happened to the two amendments that were not approved? One of them became the 27th amendment in 1992. It says that changes to lawmakers' pay can't take effect until after the next election. The second one has never been passed. It would have changed the size of the House of Representatives.

the 27th Amendment

Ninth Amendment:

Just because we made this list doesn't mean these are the only rights you have. The government can't take away any rights from people, whether they're mentioned here or not.

Tenth Amendment:

What if the Constitution doesn't give a certain power to do something? As long as it doesn't say anywhere that the states can't do something, then the states have that power.

the U.S. Constitution

CHAPTER 3

The Bill of Rights

THE STORY BEHIND THE BILL OF RIGHTS

Back when the United States was a new country, leaders from 12 of the 13 states got together. Their goal was to write a Constitution, a new set of laws for the country. Through the long, hot summer of 1787, the leaders argued about what to include in the Constitution.

the signing of the Constitution

Some leaders worried that the Constitution was missing something important. Sure, it explained the rights and responsibilities of the government. But the Constitution didn't say anything about the rights of the people. They wanted these rights to be part of the Constitution.

But even though they disagreed about some things, all but three of the leaders agreed on one thing. The country needed a stronger government. Both sides decided to sign the Constitution without a list of individual rights. They would deal with the rights issue later. On September 17, 1787, they signed the Constitution. Then they sent it to the states. They needed the approval of at least nine states before the Constitution became law.

The states held special conventions to discuss and vote on the Constitution. Two groups formed during this time. The Federalists did not think the Constitution needed a bill of rights. The Anti-Federalists disagreed.

By July 26, 1788, 11 states had approved the Constitution, making it law. But some of the states, such as Virginia, New York, and Massachusetts, wanted amendments to guarantee individual rights. They even offered lists of suggestions. And North Carolina and Rhode Island refused to approve the Constitution unless it was changed.

Crowds celebrated the approval of the Constitution.

HAMILTON

James Madison

James Madison to the Rescue

The Federalists finally gave in. The people clearly wanted a bill of rights. When Congress met for the first time, James Madison from Virginia took charge. Madison looked at the lists of rights from the states. He used that information as he wrote his list.

Madison started with a list of 17 amendments. Throughout the summer of 1789, lawmakers discussed and argued about Madison's list. Finally, Congress approved 12 of the amendments. Now it was up to the states.

Virginia's Declaration of Rights

On November 20, 1789, New Jersey became the first state to approve the amendments. Virginia, the last, approved them on December 15, 1791. States approved 10 of the 12 amendments. These 10 amendments became known as the Bill of Rights.

Today, the original Bill of Rights is preserved and protected. You can visit the document at the National Archives in Washington, D.C. The Bill of Rights is displayed with the Declaration of Independence and the Constitution. Together, these documents are known as the Charters of Freedom.

The Bill of Rights is more than 200 years old. But the ideas it describes are still just as meaningful today. What was important then is still important today. And the Bill of Rights will always be here to protect your rights.

Saving History

The government goes to great lengths to save important documents like the Bill of Rights. Cases protecting the Charters of Freedom are made of thick glass. Inside the cases, special green lights shine on the documents. The green lights keep the documents from crumbling or fading.

The glass cases also have computers that monitor the building. If there is a fire, the computer automatically moves the documents to a fireproof vault 6 feet (1.8 meters) below ground. The vault is built with metal strong enough to withstand a bomb blast. Those are some well-protected pieces of paper, aren't they?

the Bill of Rights today

The Revolutionary War begins.

Delegates at the Constitutional Convention sign the Constitution and send it to the states for approval.

April 19, 1775

September 17, 1787

1783

July 4, 1776

July 26, 1788

The Continental Congress approves the Declaration of Independence.

New York becomes the 11th state to approve the Constitution.

The Revolutionary War ends. The United States of America is officially its own country.

After being approved, the Constitution is put into place. This new form of government divides power into the executive, judicial, and legislative branches.

New Jersey becomes the first state to approve the amendments.

1788

November 20, 1789

1789

December 15, 1791

James Madison, a Representative from the state of Virginia, begins writing the Bill of Rights.

Virginia becomes the last state to approve the amendments. The Bill of Rights is added to the Constitution.

Why Do I Care?

5. People can have different opinions, and that's okay. The Bill of Rights allows U.S. citizens to say what they think without fear of arrest.

4. We can get good ideas from everyone. James Madison looked at many different sources to get ideas for the Bill of Rights.

3. Change and improvement are important in life. The Bill of Rights improved the Constitution.

2. It's important to compromise. Even though the Federalists and the Anti-Federalists didn't always agree, they still worked together for the good of the people.

1. Governments need to look out for their citizens. The Bill of Rights made sure the rights of U.S. citizens would always be protected.

Translation Guide

bear arms — We're not talking about wearing sleeveless shirts. We're not even talking about having arms like a grizzly bear. In the Bill of Rights, to bear arms means to have weapons.

due process — Due process is not the process of checking out a book from the library. Due process is the established rules and steps in legal proceedings.

jeopardy — In addition to being the name of a popular game show, jeopardy means a risk or danger.

quarter — This has nothing to do with coins. To quarter soldiers means to give them a place to sleep and eat.

redress — Redress means to get dressed again. Just kidding! Redress means to help or fix a problem.

Glossary

amendment (uh-MEND-muhnt) — a change that is made to a law

bail (BAYL) — a sum of money paid to a court to allow someone accused of a crime to be set free until his or her trial

grand jury (GRAND JU-ree) — a group of people that meet to decide if there is enough evidence to try someone for a crime

impartial (im-PAR-shuhl) — fair and not favoring one person or point of view over another

infringe (in-FRINJ) — to take away little by little

militia (muh-LISH-uh) — a group of citizens who are trained to fight, but who only serve in an emergency; today, the National Guard serves as the militia for the United States.

probable cause (PROB-uh-buhl KAWZ) — a really good reason for believing that someone should be charged with a crime

seizure (SEE-zhur) — the act of taking something away from someone

Internet Sites

FactHound offers a safe, fun way to find Internet sites related to this book. All of the sites on FactHound have been researched by our staff.

Here's how:
1. Visit *www.facthound.com*

2. Choose your grade level.

3. Type in this book ID **1429619287** for age-appropriate sites. You may also browse subjects by clicking on letters, or by clicking on pictures and words.

4. Click on the **Fetch It** button.

FactHound will fetch the best sites for you!

Read More

Donnelly, Karen J. *The Bill of Rights*. A Primary Source Library of American Citizenship. New York: Rosen Central Primary Source, 2004.

Price, Sean. *Designing America: The Constitutional Convention*. American History through Primary Sources. Chicago: Raintree, 2008.

Smith, Rich. *The Bill of Rights: Defining Our Freedoms*. The Bill of Rights. Edina, Minn.: Abdo, 2008.

Taylor-Butler, Christine. *The Bill of Rights*. True Book. New York: Children's Press, 2008.

Index